HAGGAI

HAGGAI

Stephen Kaung

Christian Fellowship Publishers, Inc.
New York

Copyright © 2022
Christian Fellowship Publishers, Inc.
New York
All Rights Reserved.

Paperback ISBN: 978-1-68062-140-2
Large Print ISBN: 978-1-68062-154-9
eBook ISBN: 978-1-68062-141-9

Available from the Publishers at:

11515 Allecingie Parkway
Richmond, Virginia 23235
www.c-f-p.com

Printed in the United States of America

Preface

Haggai prophesied for four months, taking three different days to speak five short utterances. Though he began when he was an old man, Haggai's brief prophecies helped the remnant of Israel finish re-building the temple.

In I Corinthians 14, we are told that a prophecy speaks words to edify, encourage, and comfort (see v.3). In this volume, Stephen Kaung goes through Haggai's two chapters in these three prophetic ways. He sees Haggai encouraging us first by a challenge not to give up but to repent and begin again to build. This will please and glorify the Lord. Then there are words of comfort for us in our small work, letting us know how it is all part of His great house. And finally, Haggai prophecies words to edify us, letting us know of His blessing and assuring us of His presence.

Have you heard the call to rebuild the house of God? Have you given up much for that purpose? Have you come back to Jerusalem, to that simplicity which is in Christ? Have you laid the foundation which is nothing but Christ? You have done well. But to build the house of God is not an easy job. You cannot expect that the enemy will allow you to go on smoothly without any interference. You need to hear the prophetic words of God to be strengthened for the task.

Contents

Note

The author delivered this series of messages in January 1974, before a group of Christians gathered for worship in Richmond, VA. The texts of these messages were recorded and later transcribed. Some portions of the recordings were missing and filled in using the author's preparatory notes. These notes also included several gold nuggets missing in the messages but now included in this volume.

Unless otherwise indicated,
Scripture quotations are from the
New Translation by J. N. Darby.

1—Prophetic Ministry During Recovery

II Chronicles 36:15-16—And Jehovah the God of their fathers sent to them by his messengers, rising up early and sending; because he had compassion on his people and on his dwelling-place. But they mocked at the messengers of God, and despised his words, and scoffed at his prophets, until the fury of Jehovah rose against his people, and there was no remedy.

Haggai 1:1-5—In the second year of Darius the king, in the sixth month, on the first day of the month, came the word of Jehovah by the prophet Haggai unto Zerubbabel the son of Shealtiel, governor of Judah, and to Joshua the son of Jehozadak, the high priest, saying,

Thus speaketh Jehovah of hosts, saying, This people say, The time is not come, the time that Jehovah's house should be built. And the word of Jehovah came by Haggai the prophet, saying, Is it time for you that ye should dwell in your wainscoted houses, while this house lieth waste? And now thus saith Jehovah of hosts: Consider your ways.

We would like to consider together the prophet Haggai and see what his prophetic ministry meant to the history of recovery. But before we go into the book of Haggai, we should probably lay a little bit of a foundation about prophetic ministry.

The History of Recovery

In the recovery period of the Old Testament, the remnant of the children of Israel returned to Jerusalem from Babylon. They rebuilt the temple under Zerubbabel and beautified it under Ezra. Then after many years, the wall of Jerusalem was rebuilt under Nehemiah. At that time, the order of the city of Jerusalem was also restored. All these events are history, but behind history, God's principles have never changed.

Today, God is still doing the work of recovery among His people. He is now recovering something spiritual, not physical. The spiritual temple must be rebuilt. The spiritual line or lineage of God's people with God must be restored. This must be recovered both in our individual lives with God and in our life together as a people with God. As we read in I Peter 2,

> [we] as living stones, are being built up a spiritual house, a holy priesthood, to offer spiritual sacrifices acceptable to God by Jesus Christ (2:5).

The temple must be rebuilt. We must be built up together as a spiritual house so God can dwell among us. This must take place in order for His name to be exalted, that He may receive the worship that belongs to Him, that we may serve Him as priests, that He may be satisfied. Our life with God together must be restored.

It is not only the spiritual temple that must be rebuilt, but also the spiritual wall of Jerusalem that must be restored. The whole city must be restored. Living together with God needs to be restored as well as living with one another—"Behold, how good and how pleasant it is for brethren to dwell together in unity!" (Psalm 133:1)

We believe that God is doing the work of recovery in our time, to recover our life with God and to recover our life with one another. It is only when these two sides are recovered that the testimony of Jesus will be established on this earth.

We have the historical record of this recovery with Israel in the Bible's two books: Ezra and Nehemiah. Then we have three other books that give us the prophetic utterances during this recovery: the book of Haggai, the book of Zechariah, and the book of Malachi.

Prophecies—messages sent directly from God to His people—played a very prominent part in the history of recovery. Without these prophetic messages, recovery could not be accomplished. It was through the prophecies of Haggai and Zechariah that the building of the Second Temple was eventually completed. Since we have considered the *historical* aspect of recovery[1], it

---

[1] For Stephen Kaung's ministry on the historical aspect of recovery, see *Nehemiah* published in 2020.—Publisher

would be a loss if we neglected the *prophetic* part of God's recovery work.

The Prophets: Messengers of God

Whenever God works, He raises up three different orders or offices:

the prophet, the priest, and the king

These are the three ministrations that God raises up among His people. The prophet is to speak the mind of God. The priest is to serve God. The king is to govern or rule for God. Priesthood and kingship are permanent orders. But strange to say, prophets are temporary orders. In other words, God raises up prophets that His mind may be made known to His people, but "prophecy will pass away" while kingship and priesthood will continue even into eternity.

We are redeemed by the precious blood of our Lord Jesus. He has not only washed our sins away, but He has made us kings and priests. We are to serve Him, to rule for Him, not only now in the spiritual sense, but even in the age to come. And then, even in the eternity to come (see Revelation 1:6; 5:10; 20:6).

When you read the last two chapters of the book of Revelation, you find that the church is serving God as priests and kings, but there are no more prophets. Prophets are very important today, but the day will come when all prophecies will be completed and fulfilled. There will be no more prophets in the future, but we shall serve the Lord as kings and priests forever and ever.

the class of prophets

In a very general sense, all the patriarchs were prophets. For example, Abraham was a prophet. Isaac, Jacob, Moses, even David was a prophet in a very general sense. These patriarchs were all prophets, yet prophets eventually formed a class of themselves in a more specific sense. Historically speaking, this class of prophets began with Elijah—the representative of all prophets—and it ended with John the Baptist. In Matthew 11, Jesus said, "For all the prophets and the law have prophesied unto John [the Baptist]"(v. 13).

In the New Testament time, there are also prophets, but they are not technically this class of prophets in the Old Testament. In Ephesians 4, we read that God

> has given [to the church] some apostles, and some prophets, and some evangelists, and some shepherds and teachers, for the perfecting of the saints; with a view to the work of the ministry, with a view to the edifying of the body of Christ (v.11-12).

Prophets during spiritual declension

In the history of the children of Israel, especially when they were falling away from God, you find God raised up many prophets to tell them of His thoughts and plans for them. For example, toward the end of the history of the nation of Judah, before they were to be taken into captivity, II Chronicles 36 reads,

> And Jehovah the God of their fathers sent to them by his messengers, rising up early and sending; because he had compassion on his people and on his dwelling-place. But they mocked at the messengers of God, and despised his words, and scoffed at his prophets, until the fury of Jehovah rose against his people, and there was no remedy (vv. 15-16).

Notice that prophets seem to be specially raised up in great numbers during the time of spiritual declension. God had compassion upon His people. He wanted to restore them if they would only listen to the messengers, His prophets.

Prophecies: *Forth*telling

One more thing to observe is that we probably emphasize speaking with foreknowledge whenever we think of prophecies. We tend to believe that prophets are to predict the events that are coming in the future. We think they are to foretell what will happen afterward. But strictly speaking, prophecies in the Scripture are more *forth*telling than *fore*telling. *Forth*telling is when you speak *forth* God's mind today. *Fore*telling is when you speak about something be*fore* it happens. Basically, prophecies are to tell forth the mind of God. They are to tell what God thinks about a certain situation.

What does God think about this? How does He look upon it? What does He expect of it? And what does He want His people to do concerning it?

Prophecy is the telling forth of the mind of God—*forth*telling. It is more than just *fore*telling something that will happen in the future. There will sometimes be prophecies that foretell or predict the future, but *forth*telling is the basic meaning of prophecy.

Why is it that we tend to think of prophecy in terms of foretelling instead of forthtelling? It is because this is the way our natural mind works. There is a curiosity built into our minds. We are always curious about the future, so we think of prophecies in terms of the future. But as a matter of fact, prophecy is more concerned with the mind of God over a situation than a future event.

Prophecies tell us what God wants of His people. That is why they are so related to recovery. Prophecies are necessary so that the work of God may be recovered. God sends His prophets. He sends messengers with messages from Him. Through their prophetic utterances, the people may be encouraged, comforted, edified, and stirred up to respond to God. This is what prophecy truly is.

Prophetic Ministry Needed Today

Now, brothers and sisters, we need prophets today. Oh, how we need prophets! Would that God raise up people with vision, raise up people who know His mind, raise up people that can tell us what God thinks about us and expects of us!

Again, I do not say we need prophets who will tell us what we should do tomorrow, where to go, directing our futures. I dare not say God cannot raise up prophets to give us such futuristic prophecies, but I certainly will say that it is very extraordinary. In the New Testament time, God has given us the Holy Spirit. The Holy Spirit dwells in us, and He is to teach us in all things (see John 14:26). We do not need anybody to prophesy over us that tomorrow we should marry a certain girl. The Holy Spirit will teach you in all things. Now there are cases—I am not ruling that out completely—but this is certainly not the ordinary. The usual way of guidance should be through the direct leading of the abiding Holy Spirit.

But we do need prophets who discern the situation among God's people and who can tell us what God thinks about us and what He wants to do with us. That is what we need for the recovery of God's testimony today.

We need such prophetic ministry among us. We should ask the Lord that He raise up prophets that can tell us His mind. As they share His messages, let us respond to God that the testimony of Jesus be restored.

2—The Background of Haggai

Haggai 1:3—And the word of Jehovah came by Haggai the prophet ...

Now that we have looked into prophetic ministry in general, we can move on to the prophetic book of Haggai.

Haggai's name

We do not know much about the background of Haggai, but the name Haggai means "festive" or "festival of the Lord."

Haggai was faced with a unique situation. The remnant had returned to Jerusalem to rebuild the temple, but the work of building the temple had been stopped. It was a pathetic situation. Such pathetic things surrounded Haggai, and yet his very name tells us he is festive and joyful—the festival of the Lord.

Why could he be joyful? If all you can see is what is around you, you will surely be a man of sorrows and acquainted with grief. But if you have faith, if you can see beyond what is around you, if you can see what God intends to do, if you are joined with God in His purpose, if you have faith in God that He will do it in spite of everything, then there will be joy in your heart.

Haggai's age

> Ezra 3:12—But many of the priests and Levites and chief fathers, the ancient men that had seen the first house, wept with a loud voice, when the foundation of this house was laid in their sight; and many shouted aloud for joy.

Haggai was probably an old man at that time. He was likely among the few who saw the former temple, which Solomon built. The Babylonian captivity began in approximately 606 BC. After seventy years of captivity, the remnant returned under Zerubbabel in 536 BC. The following year they started to lay the foundation of the temple. While they were rebuilding it, they were discouraged by the opposition surrounding them. The work of rebuilding the temple was stopped for around fourteen years.

By the time Haggai began to prophesy, it was the second year of King Darius. It was around 519 or 520 BC. If Haggai had been through seventy years of captivity and then came back for another fourteen or fifteen years before he started to prophesy, he would be over eighty or ninety years old. He would have been just a child when he was taken captive.

This man Haggai most likely was among the few who saw the first temple, the temple built by Solomon. And after seventy years of captivity, his childhood impression was still very deep in his mind.

He was among the remnant that returned with the one purpose of rebuilding the temple. Now he had been back for fourteen or fifteen years, and nothing was done further than laying its foundation. You know that this old man's heart must have ached over the whole situation. For seventy years, he was in captivity and must have longed to see the temple restored. That is why he came back as an old man. But now, years and years went by, and nothing more was done for the work. I have no doubt that this old man's heart must have been exercised deeply before the Lord.

Haggai's heart

Brothers and sisters, it is true that God can raise up anybody according to His pleasure to be His messenger or prophet. This is the sovereignty of God. That is true. But it is also true that if your heart is exercised before the Lord, if you inquire of the Lord, if you seek to know His mind, then God will call you to be His prophet and reveal himself to you. Why is it God calls this one to be a prophet and not that one? One is seeking, even as we are told in I Corinthians 14, to seek the great gift—that of prophecy.

Why should God call an old man to be a prophet at that moment? We would say he is too old to be of any use. Usually, it is true that if God wants to use a person, He will start with that person when he is young. That is true. But that does not rule out the older people. Thank

God for Haggai! This gives the older people some encouragement.

When we hear someone encouraging the young people, the old people sometimes sit there and think, "Well, probably we have passed out of usefulness." Not so! Here was Haggai. He must have been in his eighties or nineties. He was way beyond what people think the time of usefulness is. But notice that since this old man had a heart for the Lord, he had a vision. He was exercised before God. He sought the mind of the Lord. And if you seek the mind of the Lord, you shall know His mind.

An example of a prophet's heart—Tozer

I was asked several months ago if I believe there are still prophets today in the church. My answer was, Yes, I do believe God still raises up prophets in the church. God "gave" to the church "some prophets." These are not in that small sense of prophesying something (see I Corinthians 14:3, 31). No, these are in the larger sense of forthtelling the mind of God to His people today. God does, at times, raise up prophets.

Then I was asked if I could give an illustration of someone I thought was a modern prophet. Well, this prophet has passed on now, but I can tell you about him. Though I heard him only once in my lifetime, I read his books as well and feel that A. W. Tozer was a prophet. If you read his books, you too will find that he did know the mind of God.

I remember one day, as I had been reading through his books and his biography, I discovered something. Why is it that God seemed to give him the mind of God concerning His people? Because he sought God that he might know God's mind. He was not content just to give a sermon. He was not interested in entertaining God's people. He was seeking the Lord that he may know God's mind that he may speak as God's spokesman. As he sought Him in that way, God called him. Tozer is a good illustration of a prophet like Haggai. Haggai had the same principle of a prophet—his heart was exercised before God.

A prophet's question:

What is God's mind for us today?

Whether Haggai was a priest or not, I do not know. Some people think he was a priest since some theological questions were asked and answered in the book of Haggai. But that does not matter. Whether he was a Levite or not, whether he was old or young, "there is no respect of persons with God" (Romans 2:11 KJV).

What is important is: Has your heart been exercised? When you see the things around you, are you exercised before God? Do you enter into His presence and inquire of Him? Do you say "Lord, what does this mean? Does it mean that things should go on like this forever? What is Your word to Your people today? Is there any word? Do You have any message to send to

Your people? Is there any hope? Can there be any recovery?"

Brothers and sisters, this is what is essential. God's people are so concerned and occupied with small things, but one thing that needs to be exercised before God is: What is God's mind for us today? Does God have a message for us? Is He satisfied with us? If He is not satisfied, then why not? What can be done? What does God require of us that we might give Him what He wants?

We need prophets. We need vision. In the days of Eli, visions were rare, and the word was scarce because their eyes were dim, their ears were deaf (see I Samuel 3:1 ff.). How we need God to open our eyes, to open our ears, and to stir our hearts. As we are faced with the situation around us, and even within us, we should know God's mind. Is God satisfied with us? How can we satisfy Him? What is His mind? Is there any word from Him? Oh, if there is no word, we are as good as dead!

The concern of the prophet Haggai only reflected the concern of God's heart. He had compassion over His people, and that is the reason why He sent His prophet Haggai.

The Situation of Israel in Haggai's Days

Let us go back to see the situation during the days of Haggai. The children of Israel had already been taken into captivity for seventy years. Then the call came from a Gentile king, Cyrus of Persia. The royal decree was issued saying that all who are God's people may go back to Jerusalem to rebuild the temple of God. Most of the Jewish people were so content with their lives in the foreign land that they had no desire to go back to rebuild the temple.

But thank God, there was a remnant, about fifty thousand people. They were willing to be uprooted. They were willing to go through the perils of travel. They were willing to go back to Jerusalem, a city in waste. They were willing to go back to nothing in order to rebuild the temple of God. Here was a people whose sole purpose of returning was to rebuild the temple. Their purpose was certain. Their heart was pure. They went back for one thing and one thing only: to build the temple of God. They were a people set to live for God, to work for God. Everything was for God, nothing for themselves. That is why they went back. It was highly commendable!

And they wasted no time in rebuilding the temple. After arriving in Jerusalem, they came together as one people. They built the altar and offered sacrifices to God. The very next year, they started to lay the foundation. They were beginning to build the temple. They were single-minded before God.

Then something happened: opposition came from their enemies that surrounded them. These oppositions weakened their hands and so discouraged them that they stopped the work of rebuilding the temple. They had returned to rebuild the house of God, but now they had stopped working altogether. Why? Did they forget why they had come back? No, of course they remembered. Did they really give up the hope of rebuilding the temple? No, no. They only said one thing: "This is not the *time* to build the house of God." They did not forget to rebuild the temple. They did not give up building the house. They simply said, "This is not the time. Let's wait until it is more convenient. Then we will finish our job." In other words, they rationalized the whole thing. If they were to give up building the house of God, their conscience would not allow them to be at peace. That is why they rationalized, "This is not the time. We have not given up. It is just not the right time. We will still do it when the time comes."

Somehow their consciences were appeased. Notice the subtlety of it. Human life is such that you have to be occupied one way or another. You cannot be completely at leisure. Even when you are at leisure, you make leisure your occupation. You must be occupied. If you are not occupied with building the temple, then you will be occupied with something else. Since they were not occupied with building the temple throughout these fourteen years, what did they do? They *had* to be occupied; they *needed* to be occupied; they *wanted* to be occupied—so they started to build their own houses.

What kind of houses did they build? The Bible says that they lived in their wainscoted houses. In other words, they built houses with paneled walls. These were not just temporary dwellings. They lived in luxury and enjoyed themselves. They did a lot for themselves while the house of God laid in waste.

In the beginning, after they stopped building the temple, they told themselves they were just waiting for *the right time*. When they saw the temple was in waste, their consciences still pricked them at first. But after fourteen years—after they had built their own houses of luxury and lived in them in comfort—gradually, a kind of indifference developed. They could not help it. Eventually, they could walk by and see the temple area as waste, but it was as if they saw nothing. They got used to it. That sharpness, that cleanness, that sensitivity gradually went away until a spiritual lethargy prevailed instead of their hearts for God. Still, they did not say they would not build. They were still waiting for the right time, but the time they were waiting for would never come because of their spiritual lethargy.

This was the situation at the time of Haggai's prophecy. It was a most subtle situation. If God did not send His prophet to their midst to arouse them from their state of spiritual slumber, they would go on indefinitely. They would improve their own houses and leave the house of God in waste. Gradually, they would even forget the burden of building God's house. Think of that. Why did they come back?—to rebuild the temple. But now, the whole work of recovery was in danger of being lost. Wasn't that a serious situation?

And nobody realized it. Nobody seemed to notice it. A spiritual lethargy had developed among the remnant.

There is nothing more serious with God's people—who once have seen the vision, who once have known the will of God, who once have offered themselves for God's purpose—there is nothing more serious than to have that sensitivity gradually fade away. For people who have not yet seen the vision, they need to see. But for those who have had heavenly vision, for people who have even gone a step further and returned to Jerusalem laying the foundation, their greatest danger is spiritual lethargy. That is the greatest danger. How subtle the whole thing is!

Oh, brothers and sisters, have you heard the call to rebuild the house of God? Haven't you given up much for that purpose? Haven't you come back to Jerusalem to that simplicity which is in Christ? Haven't you laid the foundation which is nothing but Christ? You would reject everything if it was not Christ. You have done well. But to build the house of God is not an easy job. You cannot expect that the enemy will allow you to go on smoothly without any interference.

The enemy of God and of man is suddenly aroused whenever he sees anyone who intends to do God's will. At that moment, he will do everything to try and discourage, distract, deceive, and attack. Is the opposition too much for you? Do you begin to say, "This is not the time. Let's wait."? If this is not the time when will be the time?

Had Jeremiah not prophesied that after seventy years of captivity, the children of Israel would go back to Jerusalem, to Judea, and rebuild the city? God did that. Why did God raise up King Cyrus to give the decree? Why did the Spirit of God stir the heart of Zerubbabel and the remnant in the first place? If this is not the time, why should the whole thing be done at all? Why not wait eighty years, a hundred years, or a hundred and fifty years?

The word has been given. The Spirit is stirring, saying, "This is the time." When we say, "This is not the time," it is because we consider ourselves too much. It is almost like when the Lord said to His disciples that He must go to Jerusalem and be killed, but He would be raised from the dead on the third day. Peter took hold of Him and said, "Lord, be kind to yourself! Consider yourself. Don't be so foolish. You do not need to do that." The Lord turned around and faced him, saying, "Satan, get thee behind Me. You mind the things of man and not the things of God" (see Matthew 16:21-23). If we consider ourselves too much, we will fall into the same trap.

He allowed the remnant to go on like this for about fourteen years. Thank God, He was patient with them. But after those years, God exercised the heart of one man—Haggai. As his heart was exercised before the Lord, as he inquired of the Lord, day after day, the word of Jehovah came to him. "In the second year of Darius the king, in the sixth month, on the first day of the month, came the word of Jehovah by the prophet Haggai" (Haggai 1:1a). God had a word for His people.

Haggai was an old man when called to prophesy. How long did he prophesy?—four months. How often?—three different days, altogether five utterances. That's all. But was God wasting something? Not at all. Even though he began to prophesy when he was quite advanced in age, though his prophesying only lasted four months, and then it was as if he disappeared—yet what was the result of those few words? The prophecies of Haggai helped the remnant to finish rebuilding the temple.

Haggai and Zechariah

God also raised up Zechariah to continue the building work. Evidently, Zechariah was a young man (so there is hope for young men too). Zechariah was a young man with a great and sanctified imagination. God seemed to have used him for a longer period. Still, there was a time of overlap and cooperation between Haggai and Zechariah.

Haggai, being an old man, did not have too much imagination in his prophecy. Whatever he said was very concise, very deep, but to the point. There was no waste of words. He spoke like a mature old man.

But, Zechariah was different. As a young man, he was fresh with an imagination that had been sanctified by the Spirit of God. There were lots of words in

Zechariah's prophecy, but they were words of God nevertheless. Through the prophecies of Haggai and Zechariah, the people were stirred to rebuild the house, thank God!

Brothers and sisters, we, too, need to hear the word of God. In the last days, people will be hungry and thirsty, not for food and water, but because of the lack of the word of God. Many words have been and are spoken, but where is the word of God today? Do we hear the voice of the Lord speaking to our spirits?

When the prophet speaks, he challenges the people. Oh, how we want to hear something very soothing! How we like to have someone tell our children that everything will be all right!—or that it does not matter! But it does matter. If we are not in the right place, if we do not have the right attitude, the right spirit, then we need to be challenged. We should be challenged. We should be pricked in our conscience.

May God not give us rest until He can rest among us, His people.

3—The First Word: Encouragement

Haggai 1:1-15—In the second year of Darius the king, in the sixth month, on the first day of the month, came the word of Jehovah by the prophet Haggai unto Zerubbabel the son of Shealtiel, governor of Judah, and to Joshua the son of Jehozadak, the high priest, saying,

Thus speaketh Jehovah of hosts, saying, This people say, The time is not come, the time that Jehovah's house should be built. And the word of Jehovah came by Haggai the prophet, saying, Is it time for you that ye should dwell in your wainscoted houses, while this house lieth waste? And now thus saith Jehovah of hosts: Consider your ways. Ye have sown much, and bring in little; ye eat, but are not satisfied; ye drink, but are not filled with drink; ye clothe yourselves, but there is none warm; and he that earneth wages earneth wages for a bag with holes. Thus saith Jehovah of hosts: Consider your ways. Go up to the mountain and bring wood, and build the house, and I will take pleasure in it, and I will be glorified, saith Jehovah. Ye looked for much, and behold it was little; and when ye brought it home, I blew upon it. Wherefore? saith Jehovah of hosts. Because of my house that lieth waste, whilst ye run every man to his own house. Therefore over you the heavens withhold their dew, and the earth withholdeth its fruit. And I called for a drought upon the land, and upon the mountains, and upon the corn, and upon the new wine, and upon the oil, and upon that which the ground bringeth forth, and upon man, and upon cattle, and upon all the labour of the hands.

And Zerubbabel the son of Shealtiel, and Joshua the son of Jehozadak, the high priest, and all the remnant of the people, hearkened to the voice of Jehovah their God, and the words of Haggai the prophet, according as Jehovah their God had sent him, and the people feared before Jehovah. Then spoke Haggai, Jehovah's messenger, in Jehovah's message unto the people, saying, I am with you, saith Jehovah. And Jehovah stirred up the spirit of Zerubbabel the son of Shealtiel, governor of Judah, and the spirit of Joshua the son of Jehozadak, the high priest, and the spirit of all the remnant of the people; and they came and worked at the house of Jehovah of hosts, their God, in the four and twentieth day of the sixth month, in the second year of Darius the king.

On the first day of the sixth month of the second year of King Darius, the word of God came to Haggai to speak to Zerubbabel, the son of Shealtiel, governor of Judah, and to Joshua, the son of Jehozadak, the high priest. These two were the leaders. By speaking to them, God was also challenging all the remnant of His people.

There was a controversy between God and His people. The controversy did not concern the whole nation of Israel. He was not just speaking to His people in general since those in Babylon seemed to be having a good time. They could live in peace. They could do anything they liked, and God was silent with them. God said, "Let them go." But God had a controversy with the remnant. Why? Because they were the people God's eyes were upon.

The time is not come

The controversy between God and the remnant was this:

> Thus speaketh Jehovah of hosts, saying, This people say, The time is not come, the time that Jehovah's house should be built. And the word of Jehovah came by Haggai the prophet, saying, Is it time for you that ye should dwell in your wainscoted houses, while this house lieth waste? And now thus saith Jehovah of hosts: Consider your ways (vv. 2-5).

The whole controversy was over a matter of time, not a matter of purpose. Why? Because the remnant knew God's purpose. They had not given up on building the house. That is why they came back in the first place. It was just a matter of time. They said, "This is not the time." But God said, "Is this not the time for you? When will it be the right time for you? Remember that you are a committed people."

Brothers and sisters, if you are committed to God, God's time is your time. Your time is God's time. If you are committed to God, you cannot say, "This is not the time for God, but it is time for me." There is no such thinking. You are committed to God. If it is God's time, it is your time. If it is your time, it is God's time. The time is now, right now.

In these prophetic utterances, God wanted them to seek Him. He wanted them to do one thing. God said,

Consider your ways

The word *consider* means to set your heart on your way, to think about or reflect upon it. Put your heart into it and see it through. Do not just live on as if nothing is happening. Do not be indifferent, but consider your ways. Stop, think, and put your heart in it so you can discover what He says.

God said, "Consider your ways" two times, but these two times are different. The first time God said, "Consider your ways" was negative; the second time was positive.

Ye have sown much, and bring in little

In the first time that God said, "Consider your ways," what were they to consider?

> Ye have sown much, and bring in little; ye eat, but are not satisfied; ye drink, but are not filled with drink; ye clothe yourselves, but there is none warm; and he that earneth wages earneth wages for a bag with holes (v. 6).

God said, "Through the years, you sowed much, but you reaped little. You eat a lot, but you are still hungry. You drink, but your thirst is not quenched. You put on clothing, but you do not get the warmth from it. You earn wages, but the wages disappear as if they were put in a bag with holes."

Why was this happening? Since they had left off the building of the house of God and were now building their own houses, God's disciplinary hand was upon them. It is strange to say, but they did not know it. How can a person be under God's discipline and not even notice it? This shows where their hearts were.

Those who were supposed to live for God, to work for God, were now living for themselves and working for themselves. They were just like those who did not return to Jerusalem. Instead of building God's house, they were building their own houses. God could not allow this to continue, so His disciplinary hand was upon them. They sowed much, but they got little. They tried to enjoy, but they could not enjoy. Oh, brothers and sisters, if you are committed to God, He will not allow you to enjoy the world as other people do. Thank God for that!

But the strangest thing is that they did not even notice it. They ate much, but they were still hungry. They knew they did not get the warmth from the clothing. They knew they sowed much but received little. Year after year, again and again, this happened, yet their spiritual sensitivity was not aroused. They did not perceive it. Isn't that pathetic? How many of God's children today are in similar situations? They are under God's disciplinary hand, and yet they are not aware of their condition. All they have is the question—why? "Why is it we are not satisfied? Why is it?" But they do not see the hand of God.

The word came to them in answer, "Consider your ways. Why do all these things happen? Because you run to your own houses and leave the house of God in ruins. That is why." God said, "My hand is upon you. I am trying to bring you to your senses, but you are so dull. You do not understand. You do not know."

If you are committed to God, He will never allow you to be satisfied with anything else, with anything less than himself and His purpose. Is this because He does not love you? No, it is because you are one with Him. This is the first thing they are called to consider.

Go up to the mountain and bring wood ...

The second time that they are called to *consider their ways* deals with the situation in a more positive way, going forward with the Lord.

> Go up to the mountain and bring wood, and build the house, and I will take pleasure in it, and I will be glorified, saith Jehovah (v.8).

God said, "What you should do now is this, if you see that my hand is upon you, go up to the mountain and bring wood and start the work of building My house. Then I will be pleased with it, and I will be glorified."

On the one hand, we need to consider our ways to see how we have drifted away. We must see that because of our drifting, we are now under His discipline. On the other hand, once we have repented, we should go to the mountain. In other words, we should climb high. We should go to the Lord and have fellowship with Him. There we will gather the materials from Him to build the house so that God may be pleased and glorified.

What was the purpose of the remnant's return to Jerusalem?—to please God and glorify Him with a temple. That was the one purpose of their lives, but they forgot. What is the purpose of our life? Is it not to please God and glorify Him? Is there anything more honorable than that? God said, "Do it. Now do it. And the Lord will be pleased and will be glorified." Thank God!

If God should keep silent, then we are really in opposition. I cannot think about being in opposition with God, but as long as God still speaks to us, there is hope.

All the remnant ... hearkened to the voice of Jehovah their God

God began to stir up the remnant of Israel. Oh, it was the Spirit of God, not the human words of Haggai, that stirred them up. It was the word of the Lord, and the Spirit of God behind the word, that stirred Zerubbabel and Joshua and all the remnant.

> And Zerubbabel the son of Shealtiel, and Joshua the son of Jehozadak, the high priest, and all the remnant of the people, hearkened to the voice of Jehovah their God, and the words of Haggai the prophet, according as Jehovah their God had sent him, and the people feared before Jehovah (v.12).

As soon as they responded, the second word came on that very day to Haggai:

I am with you, saith Jehovah

Brothers and sisters, in one sense, He is always with us. Hasn't He said, "I will never leave you nor forsake you?" (see Hebrews 13:5b) In one sense, He is always with us. He has never left us. But in another sense—so far as our experience goes, not our position—sometimes we lose His presence. Why?—because we are not with Him. If we are with Him, He is with us! The Lord said, "Abide in me, and I abide in you" (see John 15:4). If we are with Him, we will be given the assurance that He is with us. His presence goes with us. If He is with us, if His presence goes with us, we do not need to worry anymore. We are in His will. Whatever He has called you to do, He is faithful. He will come and finish it. He is the finisher. By the strength of this promise, the remnant rose up and put their hands to the work of rebuilding the temple.

Here we see how prophetic ministry helps God's people to perform His will. Oh, may God raise up many prophets! Moses said, "would that all Jehovah's people were prophets, and that Jehovah would put his Spirit upon them!" (Numbers 11:29b) How good that would be!

4—Review

Before we consider the second occasion of Haggai's prophecy, we should remember the background and the first occasion of his prophecy.

We mentioned before that we find the history of the recovery among the people of Israel in the two books: Ezra and Nehemiah. We read how God allowed His people to return to Jerusalem to rebuild the house, the temple. Then also to rebuild the wall of Jerusalem so that the testimony of God might be re-established on earth. But the prophetic part of the recovery was to be found in three books in the Old Testament—the books of Haggai, Zechariah, and Malachi.

If we want to know God's work of recovery among His people, we should not only study the historical books about recovery, but we should also study the prophetic books. Prophecy occupies a very important place in the work of recovery. Whenever there is a declension, a falling away, a weakness, God, out of His great compassion, will send His messengers, His prophets to go to His people to restore and recover them.

There are more prophets and prophecies in a time of declension than at a normal time. Why?—because prophetic ministry is not a permanent order. Priesthood and kingship are permanent orders of God, but prophecy is a temporary order. One day prophecy will pass away, but we shall be kings and priests unto God forever and forever. But today, prophecy plays an important role in recovery. Through the prophecies of Haggai and Zechariah, the rebuilding of the temple was completed.

As we are applying these to our day, to ourselves, we find that today the testimony of Jesus is at stake. How can the testimony of Jesus be re-established on this earth? Two things are essential. First, we need to establish the life of God's people with God, as typified by the rebuilding of the temple. It is not just our individual relationship with God but our life as a people together with God that must be restored. And second, our life with one another, as typified by the rebuilding of the wall, must be restored. When these two things are recovered and restored, the testimony of Jesus will be re-established on this earth. How important the whole thing is!

For this to be accomplished, we need to hear prophetic utterances. We need to know the mind of God. We need to hear what God has to say regarding our present situation. What does He want us to do? What would please and satisfy Him? We need people with vision, sensitivity, and discernment who know the mind of God and will share with us. These people will be a great help in the work of the recovery of the testimony of Jesus.

In the case of the remnant of Israel, God raised up Haggai. Haggai was probably an old man. By this time, he might be around ninety years of age.

We often think that all the hope is with the young people, and that is usually true. But God is no respecter of persons. God can use older people as well as younger people. God used both Haggai, an older one, and Zechariah, a younger one. Through the cooperation of the old and the young, the work was done. So, we hope to encourage the older people. What is important is that they have a heart for the Lord, and they seek to know His mind.

Why did God use Haggai? Because Haggai was one who sought the mind of God. He was concerned with the situation of the remnant. He was troubled by the stoppage of the work of rebuilding the temple, and he was looking to God for a solution. As he waited upon God with his heart and spirit open, God's word came to him.

If we are open to the Lord, if we are burdened for the Lord's interest, if we inquire of Him, and if we seek to know His mind, we too shall know what His mind is, and we will be used by Him to communicate to God's people. He will use us, especially with the remnant who have responded to God, so that we all may know God's mind.

We mentioned before that Haggai prophesied for only about four months. Not only were the days of his prophecy short, but his prophetic utterances were also few in number. There were altogether five utterances that happened over three different occasions. The amount of his prophesying was short, yet the effect was great. It was through these prophetic messages that the remnant responded, and the work was done. It is not in how many words you say or how often you speak; it is whether or not God speaks through you. When God speaks, His Spirit works, and the people respond.

The first occasion of his prophetic utterances happened on the first day of the sixth month in the second year of King Darius. Through the prophet Haggai, God challenged His people. Now, remember, this challenge was not to the world. God does not challenge the world because they are not His people. God did not even challenge the whole nation of Israel. Why? Because most of the people of Israel remained in Babylon. They did not come back to Jerusalem. Instead of caring for God's interest, they cared too much for themselves. So God did not even challenge them. But God did challenge the remnant of His people—those who came back, who had the desire to stand for God. The remnant had said, "This is not the time to build the temple. Let's wait for a more convenient time, and then we will build the house of God." And God said, "Is it time for you to build your own houses? You allow the house of God to lie in waste, in ruin, and you dwell in wainscoted houses (that is, houses with paneled walls). You live in comfort, in luxury, and you allow the house of God to be in ruin? Is this the time for yourself and not the time for God?" That was the challenge.

This remnant had returned to Jerusalem for God. They were willing to be uprooted from Babylon for His sake. They came back with the one and only purpose of rebuilding the temple. And yet, they were not building the temple; they were building their own houses for about fourteen years. The longer this happened, the less sensitive their spirits became. A kind of spiritual lethargy or indifference developed among them. They had not yet completely forgotten the house of God—that was what they came back for!—and yet there was a slowness, a type of spiritual slumber among them. They could allow the house of God to lie in waste for years and years, and the longer the years, the less interested they became. That was the peril before them.

So God sent His prophet Haggai to speak to their conscience: "Is it time for you to build and dwell in your paneled houses, while it is not time for you to build My house? Consider your ways. You are under the discipline of God, and you do not know it. You labor much, you sow much, but you reap little. You eat much, but you are still hungry. You drink much, but it does not quench your thirst. You clothe yourselves much, but you do not get the warmth. You earn wages, but the wages are put in a bag with holes. Why? Why is it that you are not satisfied? Why do you drink but are never filled with drink? Why? Because you are under God's discipline. You are God's people. You have committed yourselves to God. You have committed yourself to build the house of God, and now you are building your own houses. The hand of God is upon you. He does not allow you to be fully satisfied. You should know this. You should realize it, but you are not aware of it."

Brothers and sisters, this is the danger of spiritual lethargy. We may have started out with a fresh spirit, living sensitively and seeing God's purpose, yet when we met some difficulty, we slowed down. We did not give up altogether, but gradually we developed spiritual lethargy within us. It could be that we were under God's discipline, and yet we did not know it. We wondered why we labored so much and reaped so little. We wondered why there was a spiritual drought. We wondered why God did not bless us more. We never came to realize that it was because we were under God's discipline.

Then the prophet said,

> Consider your ways. Go up to the mountain and bring wood, and build the house, and I will take pleasure in it, and I will be glorified, saith Jehovah (Haggai 1:7b-8).

God wants to arouse us from our spiritual lethargy. He wants us to be diligent in seeking His face, in gathering materials from Him, and in rebuilding the house of God.

Through this challenge, the people hearkened to the voice of God and "feared before Jehovah." Then the second word came to them, a word of comfort, of encouragement. The Lord said, "I am with you. Now go ahead. Now you are where I am. You are with Me now, and I am with you." The spirit of Zerubbabel, the spirit of Joshua and the spirit of the remnant of the people were stirred. Then on the twenty-fourth day of the sixth month—within a month—the people came together and started to build the temple.

That was the first occasion of the prophecy of Haggai. With this in mind we can now go to the second occasion of Haggai's prophecy.

5—The Second Word: Comfort

Haggai 2:1-9—In the seventh month, on the one and twentieth day of the month, came the word of Jehovah by the prophet Haggai, saying, Speak now to Zerubbabel the son of Shealtiel, governor of Judah, and to Joshua the son of Jehozadak, the high priest, and to the remnant of the people, saying, Who is left among you that saw this house in its former glory? And how do ye see it now? Is it not as nothing in your eyes? But now be strong, Zerubbabel, saith Jehovah; and be strong, Joshua son of Jehozadak, the high priest; and be strong, all ye people of the land, saith Jehovah, and work: for I am with you, saith Jehovah of hosts. The word that I covenanted with you when ye came out of Egypt, and my Spirit, remain among you: fear ye not. For thus saith Jehovah of hosts: Yet once, it is a little while, and I will shake the heavens, and the earth, and the sea, and the dry land; and I will shake all nations, and the desire of all nations shall come; and I will fill this house with glory, saith Jehovah of hosts. The silver is mine, and the gold is mine, saith Jehovah of hosts. The latter glory of this house shall be greater than the former, saith Jehovah of hosts; and in this place will I give peace, saith Jehovah of hosts.

This second time of prophesying happened about two months from the first prophetic message of Haggai. This was within a month of the time when the remnant started to do the work of building the temple. They started rebuilding the temple on the twenty-fourth day of the sixth month. And now "the word of Jehovah" came to them:

In the seventh month, on the one and twentieth day of the month

They had worked on this temple for about a month. How long did it take them to finish the building of the temple? Four years. But after they had worked on it for about a month, one thing was already clear. They did not need to wait until the temple was finished to know this thing: the temple which they are now building could never be compared with the temple built by Solomon—not by any means, there was not any chance. Within a month, they could see very clearly that what they were building could never match up with what Solomon had done, and that discouraged them.

They were thinking, "Is it worthwhile to rebuild it? It can never arrive at the glory of that temple built by Solomon. Then why bother? Is it worth it? Should we just give it up because there is no possibility of arriving at the former glory?" When they realized this, it was like a dagger stabbed into their chests.

Solomon's Temple vs. the Second Temple

Let us compare the temple built by Solomon with this temple to be rebuilt by the remnant.

Solomon spent seven years building the temple. He started in the fourth year of his reign and finished in the eleventh year (see I Kings 6:37-38). This Second Temple was completed in four years (see Ezra 4:24; 6:15).

When Solomon built the temple, he mobilized 70,000 people to bear burdens, 80,000 stone masons, and 3,600 supervisors to superintend the work (see II Chronicles 2:2). But look at the remnant. The whole number of the remnant came only to about 60,000 or less. Even if everyone worked—the men and the women, the servants, and the children, everyone would be involved in that work—it was a mere 60,000. Solomon had 70,000 just to bear the burden, 80,000 stone masons, and 3,300 supervisors. You cannot compare these two labor forces. The laborers for the Second Temple were so few.

When Solomon built the temple, he had gold in abundance, silver in great measure, and stones and timber that could not be numbered—there was no limit to his resources. But look at the measure of the remnant who were building the Second Temple. They were slaves coming back from captivity. Even if they took everything they owned and the things that were given by others, together with the few vessels that King Cyrus allowed them to bring back, those materials could not even be compared with what was in Solomon's Temple. Solomon had such abundance, while the remnant had very little.

Let us compare the size of the two temples. Solomon's Temple was majestic and gigantic. It was built with massive stones, covered with gold, with porches, and with pillars. The holy-place and the holiest-of-all were both still the same size in the Second Temple as Solomon's Temple. But the rest of the building was much smaller in comparison. Later, at the time of Christ, Herod the Great used forty-six years to enlarge the rest of the building. But at first, when the remnant built the Second Temple, it was rather small. Everything was smaller. Every area of this new temple building had no comparison to the original one which Solomon had built.

There were those still alive who had seen the former temple. Haggai was probably one of the older men who had seen it. When they looked at what they were building, their hearts sank. It seemed like nothing. God knew what was going on in their minds. God knew that even when they began to work on it, their heart was already feeling down. Therefore, within a month, the word of God came to the remnant through Haggai, saying:

> Who is left among you that saw this house in its former glory? and how do ye see it now? Is it not as nothing in your eyes? (Haggai 2:3)

They still had some among them who had seen the former glory of "this house," that is, the glory of the temple built by Solomon. Though only a few were left, they might have been talking about it, and soon everybody would have known.

What about now? How do you see things in the church? Is it not as nothing in your eyes? Oh, brothers and sisters, don't brood secretly within yourselves. God wants you to bring it out.

God knew what was going on in the minds of the returned remnant. They dared not say it, but it was eating them up within. God was not afraid to bring everything out in the open. He never wants us to deceive ourselves.

God said, "All right, if you compare what you are building now with what Solomon had built, it is nothing in your eyes, and you are right." It was nothing compared to what Solomon had built, but was it really nothing? Does God measure things by their outward appearances? Does the value of the house rest on its physical glory or spiritual glory? What really matters to God?

It is true that Solomon's Temple was majestic, built with splendor, and this temple that the remnant was building was small and less costly. If you look at the outward appearance of things, putting a value on the physical building, this was nothing. But God said, "This is not the way I look at things. I do not put a value on the physical, on the material, on the size, on the outward appearance. My value is in the spiritual aspect of it."

this house in its former glory

Notice that God did not say, "the glory of the former house." God said, "This house in its former glory." Do you see the difference? God did not say, "Have you seen the glory of the *former house*? And now you see the little, the nothing of this house." No, God did not say that. God said, "Have you seen the former glory of *this house*?" In other words, with God, there is only one house. Whether it is the tabernacle of Moses, or the temple of Solomon, or the temple rebuilt by the remnant and enlarged later by Herod the King, or the spiritual house that Christ builds today—with God, there is only one house.

Wealthy people today may have many houses. They may have a winter house or a summer cottage, but our God has only one house. He does not believe in many houses. The people may have thought that the house of Solomon was one house, and the house built by the remnant was another. God said "no" to that mindset when He called them both "this house." With God's house, there is a continuance, a unity, a oneness. The tabernacle built by Moses, the temple built by Solomon, the temple the remnant were building, and even the spiritual house that Christ is building are all just *one* house.

When He said, "this house in its former glory," it means the glory that was seen in the temple built by Solomon. That was the "former glory." What they were building was still the same house, not another one—"this house." Sometimes, the house of God may look very massive and majestic. At other times, it may not even be seen, or it may look as if it is nothing. These appearances are all part of the same house. Yes, sometimes it may look good; other times, it may look small. Sometimes it may be full of splendor, but it may not even be noticed at other times. But God said, "They are still all part of My house."

In other words, it was as if He was telling the remnant, "What you are doing is not lost. What you are doing is part of My plan. You are building My house, and that is what really matters. It does not matter how it looks outwardly. It does not matter, so long as you are involved with the building of My house. That is what really matters. Don't be discouraged."

When you read the first few chapters of the book of Acts, you see the former glory of the church, the house. And then you look and see what you are involved with today. You have the same feeling. "Why bother? There is no reason that we should glorify this building. It just will not work. It can never regain that glory that we see in Acts 1-4." But God says, "It is one house." He is building it. He does not care about the outward things so long as you are involved in the building of His house. That is what matters.

be strong ... and work: for I am with you

The Lord said, "Be strong, Zerubbabel, be strong Joshua, be strong all you people of God and work. Do not brood over these things. Do not be deceived by outward appearances. Be strong and work because this is what I want."

The Lord also said, "I am with you. I know what you are going through. This is my way. Just be faithful; that is all that I require. It is not in these outward things." Why did the Lord say this?

I will shake

Because one day everything will be shaken. God said, "I will shake the heavens and the earth, the sea and the dry land." Eventually, all that is physical will be shaken off. Don't put a value on the outward things. Sooner or later, all these outward things will be shaken to pieces. All that can be shaken will be shaken off that the kingdom which cannot be shaken may abide (see Hebrews 12:28).

This is what really matters. If we are building something big, and it is not of God, it is a deception. One day the fire will burn it (see I Corinthians 3:15). One day it will be shaken and disappear. But if it is something done in the will of God, something done out of love, something done with God, then though it may not appear to be anything, it will be there in eternity. All of the building work is part of the final New Jerusalem. The tabernacle of Moses, the temple of Solomon, and the temple rebuilt by the remnant are all part of the New Jerusalem. All that is typified from those past physical houses of God, and realized in the spiritual house, the church of God, are consummated in the holy city, the New Jerusalem.

The word ... remain[s] among you

Furthermore, in Haggai 2:5, God basically said, "I have not changed."

> The word that I covenanted with you when ye came out of Egypt, and my Spirit, remain among you: fear ye not.

I wonder what "the word" which God covenanted with the children of Israel referred to. I think it probably refers to Exodus 19:1-6:

> In the third month after the departure of the children of Israel out of the land of Egypt, the same day came they into the wilderness of Sinai: they departed from Rephidim, and came into the wilderness of Sinai, and encamped in the wilderness; and Israel encamped there before the mountain. And Moses went up to God, and Jehovah called to him out of the mountain, saying, Thus shalt thou say to the house of Jacob, and tell the children of Israel: Ye have seen what I have done to the Egyptians, and how I have borne you on eagles' wings and brought you to myself. And now, if ye will hearken to my voice indeed and keep my covenant, then shall ye be

> my own possession out of all the peoples—for all the earth is mine—and ye shall be to me a kingdom of priests, and a holy nation. These are the words which thou shalt speak to the children of Israel.

God brought Israel out of Egypt to Sinai. This was the sign God had given to Moses originally to show that it was He who sent him there. What was the sign? That the people would worship Him on that mountain, Mount Sinai (see Exodus 3:12).

God had brought His people to Mount Sinai as "on eagles' wings." God had brought His people to himself and said, "If you will hearken to my voice, if you seek my covenant, I will make you a peculiar people, a people of my possession out of all the nations, and I will make you a kingdom of priests, a holy nation."

That was what God put to the children of Israel in the first place when He took them out of Egypt. And now, with the remnant, He said, "My word and my covenant have not changed. In spite of what has happened through the years, my covenant stood, and my word stood. This is what I say, and I still keep it. I will make you a peculiar people, a special people, a nation of priests that you may serve Me."

and my Spirit, remain[s] among you

Not only has God's word not changed—not a bit—but He also said, "My Spirit remains the same." As the Spirit of God led the children of Israel out of Egypt, through the wilderness, and into the Promised Land, that same Spirit was now with the remnant. His word and His Spirit remained with them.

Brothers and sisters, what else do you want? We may change, we often change, but God's word stands forever. His covenant with us never changes, and His Spirit abides with us. With His word and with His Spirit, all things are possible. This is where our strength is: "fear ye not."

Oh, how the heart of the remnant was comforted! God said, "I remain the same with you. Just as in the beginning when I led you out of Egypt unto myself." What a comfort that is! Those who are faithful to the Lord will have His word and His Spirit to strengthen them as they go on.

the desire of all nations shall come

But you know God looks far ahead, beyond the immediate. So He said,

> Yet once, it is a little while, and I will shake the heavens, and the earth, and the sea, and the dry land; and I will shake all nations, and the desire of all nations shall come; and I will fill this house with glory, saith Jehovah of hosts (Haggai 2:6-7).

The remnant was looking at the little house they were building, and they were quite disturbed, but God said, "I am looking way ahead. Yet once, in a little while, I will shake the heavens and the earth and the sea and the dry land. I will shake *all* the nations, and the desire of the nations shall come." Now, what is "the desire of the nations"? I believe the desire of the nations is Christ.

The prophet goes further and further out to the future, and God said, "Don't be discouraged. It is true, the little you are doing is nothing physically speaking, but that does not matter because all that is physical, and the material will be shaken and fall. Even the heavens and the earth will be shaken! All these things will go away! The whole of the nations will be shaken. I will bring in My Christ—the desire of the nations. And when I bring in My Christ, I will fill this house with glory."

and I will fill this house with glory

What is this house that will be filled with glory? The same house the remnant were building would be filled with glory when Christ came. That same "little house" would be fully realized in the church.

If only the remnant could see this, they would not be discouraged. They knew that what they were doing was in line with God's divine plan. To illustrate this understanding, you could draw a straight line to show God working His plan. Then add a dip in it to show the failure of the remnant. The remnant came out of that dip and were now going back up to join that straight line. They were going forward with God's plan. Nothing was lost. It was just in the process of His plan.

That's why the Lord said, "The desire of the nations shall come, and He will fill the house with His glory."

The silver is mine, and the gold is mine

The Lord said, "Don't be so concerned that you have no gold and you have little silver. What can you do? When Solomon built the temple, there was gold and silver in great abundance. I know you would like to build with abundant gold and silver, but you do not have it. But the silver is Mine, and the gold is Mine."

Gold represents the glory and nature of God. Silver represents the redemptive work of our Lord Jesus. The house that Christ is building today—the church—is certainly built with gold and silver. There is no lack of it. He is the supplier of silver and gold. He will build the spiritual house, in which He can dwell, with gold—with His own life, His own nature, His own glory. He will also build His church with the redemptive work of Christ. Everything is based upon the redemption that our Lord Jesus has finished for us. When you come to the holy city, the New Jerusalem, you find gold all over. The Lord says, "It is Mine. I am able to supply. I am able to do it."

The latter glory of this house shall be greater than the former

Do not think back to the time of Solomon and compare the glory of the temple he built with the Second Temple. It was a fact that this Second Temple, which the remnant built, was small and less costly in every way. It could not be compared with the temple of Solomon.

There were also certain things missing in this Second Temple. The ark was missing along with the mercy seat upon it. The Shekinah glory of God was also missing. Remember that when Solomon's Temple was first established, God's glory came and rested upon the mercy seat. The Second Temple also did not have the fire that came down from heaven to burn the sacrifice when it was first built. They were also missing the Urim and the Thummim that the high priest used to wear on his breastplate so he might know the mind of God. Even after the remnant had finished their work of recovery, some of these most essential items or experiences were still missing.

Brothers and sisters, when you think of that, your heart just faints. Why bother? If that is the case, why do anything at all?

But the Lord said, "Now despite all that is lacking, the latter glory of the house shall be greater than the former glory." Yes, in Solomon's time, there was the ark, and when the ark was brought into the temple built by Solomon, and the staffs were pulled out so the ark would permanently stay there, the glory of the Lord not only filled the holiest of all, but He filled the whole temple so that even the priests could not stay and serve there. And when Solomon prayed, fire came down from heaven and burned the burnt offering on the altar. The priests at that time had the Urim and Thummim to use for making decisions. Oh, everything was glorious!

But brothers and sisters, all these were just types. The latter glory of this house will be greater than the former glory. Why? Because this house, the church, is not built with hands. It is built with living stones—His redeemed ones. This house is God's dwelling place. He will not only fill it with His glory, but He said,

in this place will I give peace

He said, "I have my rest." There is a union, not only a fitting together but a union. There is a union and communion that far surpass the former glory of this house.

Oh, brothers and sisters, to think that one day there will be the manifestation of the house that God has been building all of these centuries! All of this time has passed, and one day, when the holy city, the New Jerusalem, appears, its shining will be as the glory of God. It may seem like you are contributing little to that house, but nothing can be compared with its glory. Nothing is too hard for you when you compare it with that glory.

God said, "In this place will I give peace." There will be peace forever. Sometimes we need to be challenged. Whenever we are not where we should be, whenever we are not doing what we should be doing, we need to be exhorted and challenged. But there will be other times when we need to be comforted.

Oh, if only we answer to the Lord; if we are what He wants us to be, and do what He wills us to do! Sometimes we may be discouraged seeing "the little," it is as nothing in our hands, but the Lord is "the God of all comfort." He comforts us. The Lord knows our situation. He is working out His plan. The latter glory of this house will be greater than the former glory. When God spoke in that way to Zerubbabel, Joshua and all the house of the remnant were comforted. They were able to carry on.

May the God of all comfort, comfort His people.

Lord, You have to speak. Your Spirit has to carry a word into human hearts that we may hear, that we may be comforted. Comfort those who need to be comforted. Challenge those who need to be challenged. Oh, we do want to be where Thou dost want us to be, and we do want to be engaged in what Thou dost want us to be engaged with. Oh, Lord, have mercy upon us. We prayed, and we fasted because Thou dost not look at outward things—how big, how beautiful, how expensive. Lord, one day all these will be shaken away, but the kingdom that cannot be shaken shall remain. Oh, Lord, we want that kingdom. We want to be engaged in that work. Help us, Lord. In Thy name we pray, Amen.

6—A Threefold Prophetic Word

I Corinthians 14:3—But he that prophesies speaks to men in edification, and encouragement, and consolation.

We have been considering together the relationship of prophetic ministry to the work of recovery. God was doing the work of recovery among His people Israel. God was to recover the temple through this remnant who returned from Babylon to Jerusalem. He was to restore the walls of Jerusalem. In accomplishing such a work, prophetic ministry occupied a very important part. It was through the prophecy of Haggai and Zechariah that the temple was rebuilt.

The Work of Recovery

We do believe that God is doing a work of recovery today. Most all of God's works are the work of recovery. When you read through the whole Bible, you notice this. The first two chapters of Genesis are the initial work of God, and then starting from chapter three onward, it is all the work of recovery. Something had happened. Something had failed God, and God was out to recover to His original purpose.

We especially see this in the way the children of Israel failed God. God had raised them up as a testimony of himself on earth, but they failed God completely. Jerusalem was destroyed. The temple was destroyed. The people were taken into captivity. God was then only called "the God of the heavens" instead of "the God of the heavens and the earth." Why? There was no testimony on the earth through Israel. But God set out to recover His people, to recover Jerusalem, to recover the temple, and most of all to recover His own testimony on the earth, which was committed to His people.

Brothers and sisters, this is what God is doing today in His church. He is doing the work of recovery. He is recovering His people so they may be where they should be and what they ought to be. He is recovering their life together with God as typified by the temple. He is recovering the life of God's people one with another as represented by the rebuilding of the wall. When God's people are built up together, one with another, and as God's people serve Him as one people, then the testimony of Jesus on earth will be established. God is doing this work of recovery all the time. But in doing such a work, there needs to be prophetic ministry.

When God Speaks

When we mention prophetic ministry, we do not mean foretelling things concerning certain people or events. No, prophetic ministry essentially means that God shares His mind concerning His people and their current condition. God makes known His mind to ones who have their hearts exercised before God. He shares with them what He wants His people to do. Through the ministry of such prophets, the people of God are restored to what He expects of them. This is what prophetic ministry is.

We need to look to the Lord that He will raise up some true prophets during our current time. We need those who seek God's face, those who inquire of God as to His mind concerning His people today, those who can share with us God's mind that we may know what we should do, how we can please God, and glorify His name.

In the time of the recovery of Israel, God raised up Haggai. Evidently, he was an old man. I do want to encourage old people. Though he was probably around ninety, he was not too old; he sought God, and God raised him up as a prophet.

The time of his prophesying was rather short. It lasted only four months in which he only spoke a few times on three different occasions. On the first day of the sixth month in the second year of Darius, God's word came to him twice. On the twenty-first day of the seventh month, God's word came to him again. On the twenty-fourth day of the ninth month of the same year, God's word came to him twice. There were altogether five times on three occasions. They were all very brief, very short, but nevertheless, these were God's messages to His people. Thank God, Zerubbabel, and Joshua, and the remnant harkened to the voice of God.

It is not in the much speaking that things are accomplished. If only God will speak, then it will be done. How we need to ask the Lord that He will always speak to us! How we need to look to the Lord that we may have a ready ear to hear, we may hear what He wants us to hear and respond to Him.

We read in I Corinthians 14, a threefold description of what a prophecy is: "he that prophesies speaks to men in edification, and encouragement, and consolation." Those who prophesy speak words to edify, to encourage, and to comfort. We may say that Haggai spoke in these three ways.

Haggai's First Word—Encouragement

The first time when God's word came to Haggai, it was a challenge. God challenged His people. The people said, "It is not the time to build the house," so God challenged them by saying, "Is this the time for you to build your house? How can you live in your wainscoted [paneled] houses and allow the house of God to lie in waste for fourteen years without doing anything? Do you not realize that during these years, you labor much, but you get little? You sow a lot, but you reap little. You eat, but it does not satisfy you. You drink, but your thirst is not quenched. You dress, but you do not get warm. You earn wages, but the wages are put in a bag with holes. Do you realize what has happened to you all these years? Why is it that your life is so unsatisfying? Why is it that there is *never* a fulness? Why? Do you not know that it is because you run off to work on your own houses and allow My house to lie in ruin? Do you not know that you are under the discipline of God? Consider your ways. If only you would repent, go up to the mountain, bring down the wood, and build the temple. I will be pleased with it, and I will be glorified in it."

Brothers and sisters, where are our hearts? Is there a spiritual lethargy descending upon our spirits? Are we as keen, as sensitive to God's needs as in the beginning? Time has passed since then. Can we see the same thing happening to us? Has the vision lost its impact upon us?

Once God's people have heard His call and been given a vision of His needs, they have a new danger to watch for—spiritual lethargy. From time to time, we need to be awakened through prophetic messages. We hear His voice, consider His word in our hearts, and understand our present situation. Then we will repent and be restored to our first love.

Immediately after the spirits of the remnant were stirred, even before they set their hands to the work, God's promise came to them. He said, "I am with you." When God's word first came through Haggai to the remnant of the Jews, it was a challenge. And then it was a promise.

Haggai's Second Word—Comfort

After the Lord stirred up Zerubbabel, Joshua, and the remnant, they all began to work on the temple—on the twenty-fourth day of the sixth month. About a month later—on the twenty-first day of the seventh month—God's word came to Haggai again. Why? Because there was a real need for comfort.

It took the remnant four years to rebuild the temple, but it did not take them even a month to realize it would be different from the old temple. They could never restore the temple to the glory that was there when Solomon built it. This realization depressed and discouraged them. They realized that what their hands were building was nothing compared to the glory of Solomon's Temple. If it was going to be nothing, was it worthwhile to do it at all?

If you do not have a heart for the Lord, you can see the temple in ruins, and it is as if you have not seen it. You can pass by every day, and it doesn't bother you. But once your spirit is stirred, once your heart is set on the house of God, the temptation is to think: "If it cannot be restored to the former glory, then what is the use of doing it at all?" That mindset has become the problem.

We want to put our hands on it and restore it to the full glory of the temple built by Solomon. That is what we think we should accomplish. If this cannot be achieved and what we do can never be compared with the former glory, then why do it?

When I read Acts chapters 1-4, oh, I see the glory of the house of God!—that spiritual house, filled with glory! Then I begin to see the work of my hands, and I say, "Lord, is it worth it? If it cannot be restored to that glory, why begin? It is of no use."

So the word of God came through Haggai to the remnant to comfort them. "Who is left among you who has seen the former glory of the temple?" A few of them had seen it. Haggai probably was one of them. "And now, see what you are doing. Don't you say in your heart that it is as nothing at all?" "Oh!" God says, "Don't say it is nothing. Don't say that." Why? In the eyes of God, it is not that which is visible that is important, but that which is invisible. It is not the physical but the spiritual. It is not the outward appearance that matters but the inward reality. The temple built by Solomon was majestic, glorious in splendor, and built with precious materials in abundance. When comparing this temple which the remnant were building, it seemed to them as nothing.

God said, "I do not look at outward appearances. I do not put my value upon material things. It is the heart that I am looking into. And what is built there is of the Spirit. That is real; that will last. All the physical materials will sooner or later fade away. Yet a little while I will shake the heavens and the earth and the sea and the land—everything that is material, everything that is physical, everything that is just outward—all these things will be shaken."

The temple built by Solomon had been destroyed. This smaller temple which they were building would later be enlarged by Herod the Great. But it, too, would be destroyed in 70 AD. But that which God himself has built can never be destroyed. There is a city with foundations which God has built and that can never be destroyed (see Hebrews 11:10; 12:27).

God said, "The latter glory of this house shall be greater than the former glory." How can it be? The remnant looked at the temple they were building and it could never be compared with the glory of the first temple that was built by Solomon. But God has only one house, not many. The tabernacle built by Moses, the temple built by Solomon, the Second Temple they were building, and later on, the spiritual house that Christ would build (which is the church)—are all just one house. It is the "latter glory of *this* house"—one house. Eventually, all will be consummated in the holy city, the New Jerusalem. What will remain there? Not the gold and silver that Solomon put into the temple. Instead, it is the gold of the nature of God; it is the silver of the redemption of Christ. Those will be found in the holy city, the New Jerusalem. What you can see is not important. Do not be discouraged. Even this little house, though it's almost nothing, if it is done in the right spirit, if it is done for the glory of God, if it is done in the will of God, then it is part of "this house" and will count for eternity. Oh, brothers and sisters! If only you could see that, you would never be discouraged. God comforted them with that second word. It was a word of comfort.

Haggai's Third Word—Edification

As we read in I Corinthians 14, those who prophesy speak to men to edify, encourage, and comfort. We may say the first word that came through Haggai to God's people was the word of encouragement. God encouraged them to start the building of the house. The second time the word of God came to Haggai, a month later, was the word of consolation or comfort. God was comforting His people through prophetic utterance. And next, we will see how God's word came to Haggai for the third time as a word of edification in the ninth month. It was an edifying word for building up the remnant of Israel.

7—The Third Word: Edification

Haggai 2:10-23—On the four and twentieth day of the ninth month, in the second year of Darius, came the word of Jehovah by Haggai the prophet, saying, Thus saith Jehovah of hosts: Ask now the priests concerning the law, saying, If one bear holy flesh in the skirt of his garment, and with his skirt do touch bread, or pottage, or wine, or oil, or any food—shall it become holy? And the priests answered and said, No. And Haggai said, If one that is unclean by a dead body touch any of these, is it become unclean? And the priests answered and said, It shall be unclean. Then answered Haggai and said, So is this people, and so is this nation before me, saith Jehovah, and so is every work of their hands; and that which they offer there is unclean. And now, I pray you, consider from this day and onward, from before a stone was laid upon a stone in the temple of Jehovah,—before those days were, when one came to a heap of twenty measures, there were but ten; when one came to the vat to draw out fifty press-measures, there were but twenty. I smote you with blasting and with mildew and with hail in all the work of your hands; and ye turned not to me, saith Jehovah. Consider, I pray you, from this day and onward, from the four and twentieth day of the ninth month, from the day that the foundation of God's temple was laid, consider it. Is the seed yet in the barn? Yea, the vine, and the fig-tree, and the pomegranate, and the olive-tree have not brought forth: from this day will I bless you.

Now we come to the third occasion of the prophecy of Haggai. Haggai first started to prophesy on the first day of the sixth month in the second year of King Darius. Then the remnant started to rebuild the temple on the twenty-fourth of the same month. The second word came on the twenty-first day of the seventh month. And now this third word was given on

the four and twentieth day of the ninth month, in the second year of Darius

So the remnant had been working on the temple for about three months now.

The ninth month is the time for winter sowing. In our calendar, this will be either in November or December. The children of Israel in the Promised Land sowed the winter seed and expected the latter rain. If they had an abundance of latter rain, they would have a good harvest.

This ninth month, the time for winter sowing, was an important time. Why? Because before this time, God had sent them a drought. The land was dry. There was no rain. The situation in the land of Israel was so peculiar. True, it was a land "flowing with milk and honey," and yet it depended on rain completely. If there should be rain, the land would be abundant. If there should be no rain, then the earth would turn into dust, and there would be nothing.

Why did God bring them to such a place? A land flowing with milk and honey and yet completely dependent upon the rain from heaven? Because God wanted His people to depend upon Him. God said, "If you keep My word, there will be rain, but if you do not keep My word, I will shut up the heavens. Then you will see what will happen."

Now the remnant came back to Jerusalem and the neighboring cities. They came back to build the temple, but God still sent them a drought. Why? Because they stopped building the temple and began to build their own houses. They sowed their seed and hoped to reap, but there was no rain. They were under the disciplinary hand of God.

They had now come to their senses. They started to rebuild the temple. It had already been three months, but there was still no rain. As they began to sow the winter seed, they wondered whether God would send the rain.

Expected Blessings

According to the law, God would bless them if they should keep His word and covenant. God would bless their crops, fields, cattle, and sheep and give them plenty of food. There would be no lack of bread. God would give them plenty of rain. This was God's promised blessing to His people (see Deuteronomy chapters 6 and 28). God said, "If you keep My word, if you are faithful to Me, then I will bless you." There are many blessings and among those blessings was the blessing of nature. But God also said, "If you are unfaithful, then the curse will be upon you."

So they had been under a kind of curse, and now they responded to God. They had put their hand into the work for three months and sown the winter seed. Still, nothing happened. They began to question. "Now what? Was it all really God's discipline, or was it just a coincidence? We have returned to God. Will God return His blessings to us?" As they were working on the temple, maybe they were also looking at the sky and wondering what would happen. We must understand how they felt at that time. Then the word came through Haggai to build up their faith.

Since the children of Israel were an earthly people of God, all God's promises and blessings were earthly. If they obeyed God, God would bless them with abundant food, a big family, and make them the first of the nations—all earthly blessings. As God's earthly people, they expected such blessings. If such blessings did not come, something must be wrong. If God was faithful, then their faithfulness was in question because they were God's earthly people. Since they had now been faithful to the Lord for three months, they were daily expecting God's blessings to come upon them.

When God's blessings were withheld, they began to wonder and question why.

Spiritual Blessings

Dear brothers and sisters, who are we? Are we God's earthly people? No, we are God's heavenly people. God promised Abraham that his seed would be as the sand on the seashore and as the stars in heaven. In a sense, the children of Israel were the sand of the sea, and we are the stars of heaven. As a heavenly people of God, God has also promised us His blessings. And what are they? Ephesians 1 says,

> Blessed be the God and Father of our Lord Jesus Christ, who has blessed us with every spiritual blessing in the heavenlies in Christ (v.3).

God has blessed us with every spiritual blessing in the heavenlies in Christ Jesus. Nothing is missing.

Should we expect God to bless our barn, to bless our field, to bless our business, to make us prosperous, wealthy, or even great in this world? Should we expect God's blessing in these physical ways? We do not say God will not bless us in those ways. Those blessings do come, but only alongside the spiritual blessings:

> But seek ye first the kingdom of God and his righteousness, and all these things shall be added unto you (Matthew 6:33).

Physical blessings happen, but they are not the main blessings. The blessings that God has promised us are spiritual blessings.

If we obey the Lord, if we follow Him wholeheartedly, there will be much fruit in our field, the fruit of the Spirit—"love, joy, peace, long-suffering, kindness, goodness, fidelity, meekness, self-control" (Galatians 5:22-23). If we really love the Lord, there will be no lack of spiritual children, grandchildren, and great-grandchildren. There will be much increase of the life of Christ in us. These are all spiritual blessings.

I am afraid that today God's people are trying to go back to the old covenant relationship with Him as they seek physical blessings. They would rather be God's earthly people than God's heavenly people.

Dependence on His Blessings

> I will not let thee go except thou bless me (Genesis 32:26b).

Should we expect God to bless us? We should. We cannot live without His blessings. Before we knew God, we could live without His blessings. We did not need Him. But now, since we know Him, we cannot live without His blessings. We need Him. We have to depend on Him.

At first, Jacob could live by himself. He could use his own cleverness to accumulate his wealth. But when God touched his thigh, and he was crippled, he held on to the Angel of the Lord and said, "Bless me, or I will not let You go." Why? "I am crippled. Without Your blessing, I cannot live anymore."

Oh, brothers and sisters, as God's people, we should expect God's blessings. Why? Because we depend on God. If He does not bless us, we can do nothing. It is a life of dependence upon God. But in looking for God's blessing, we do not look for earthly things. These may be added, but these are not the main thing. In looking for God's blessings, we should look to the Lord that Christ may be increased in us, that His nature may be formed in us, that He may use us for the furtherance of His kingdom and His righteousness, that we may be fruitful on every side. These are the blessings we should look to the Lord for. And when the blessings are withheld, it is time for us to examine ourselves before the Lord, asking, "Why is it the blessing is withheld?"

God's Testing of Our Faith

After the children of Israel had been faithful to the Lord for three months, it was time for them to question God. So God answered them by telling Haggai to ask the priests—who were to explain, interpret, and apply the law—two theological questions concerning the law.

Thus saith Jehovah of hosts:
Ask now the priests concerning the law

Now, brothers and sisters, I have meditated much on these two questions, and I will try to explain a little bit, but I have to say I am not satisfied fully. May the Lord show us more.

Question One

> If one bear holy flesh in the skirt of his garment, and with his skirt do touch bread, or pottage, or wine, or oil, or any food—shall it become holy? And the priests answered and said, No (Haggai 2:12).

According to Leviticus 6, the holy meat that touches anything makes that thing holy. So the holy meat, being in the skirt, sanctifies the skirt. But the sanctified skirt cannot sanctify the food that the skirt touches. Do you see the point? The holy meat does sanctify the skirt, but the skirt cannot sanctify any meat or food that it touches. The answer from the priests was right according to the law.

Question Two

> And Haggai said, If one that is unclean by a dead body touch any of these, is it become unclean? And the priests answered and said, It shall be unclean (Haggai 2:13).

According to the law, if a dead body defiles a person, he is unclean for seven days—that is, only if he went through purification. It took seven days of purification to be cleansed. If he did not go through the purification process, then he would be excommunicated from the congregation of Israel.

The Meaning of the Questions

What do these two questions and answers mean? I do not know for certain, but I think we can understand something about them. The holy meat can make holy the skirt that it touches, but holiness does not go beyond the skirt. But if someone becomes unclean through a dead body, that uncleanness goes much further. Under the law, uncleanness has a greater impact than holiness. Why? Because holiness under the law is an outward thing. But uncleanness touches the inward nature of a person.

In the New Testament, holiness is no longer an act; it is a Person. Christ is our holiness, and if Christ is our holiness, He not only makes us holy, but if we touch anybody, we can assert our impact of holiness. Why? Because it is inward. But under the law, it is outward. So under the law, you find these evil effects of uncleanness are greater than holiness's good effect. That probably is a reason for these questions.

The Application of the Questions

Another reason for these questions is because of their application. We do not understand the two parables, but we know the application. Why? Because God's word came to Haggai and said,

> So is this people, and so is this nation before me, saith Jehovah, and so is every work of their hands; and that which they offer there is unclean (v.14).

What does it mean? They offered sacrifices, and they were considered a holy nation because they offered sacrifices. But God looks upon the heart. Even though they did offer sacrifices and were considered a holy nation, their hearts were not circumcised. They were defiled by "the dead body"—the flesh. Outwardly, they offered, they were positionally known as a holy nation, but inwardly they still lived in the flesh and were unholy and unclean. They came back to Jerusalem to build the house, they were like the skirt that could wrap the holy meat, but they left the house of God in ruins and went about their own business. Their heart was not pure. God did not go by outward things; God went by their inward hearts.

... so is this nation before me ...
so is every work of their hands;
and that which they offer there is unclean

God said that anything they touched was unclean. Before "a stone was laid upon a stone in the temple," when they went to a heap of twenty measures, they only got ten. They went to a vat of fifty press-measures, but there were only twenty. God sent mildew and hail to break it up because everything was unclean in His sight.

Well, in their hearts, they said, "God, haven't we been faithful for three months already? And shouldn't Thy blessing now come upon us?" God said, "Yes."

from this day will I bless you

When they returned to the Lord, God's blessings returned to them, but there was a testing period. These three months were months of testing. They expected that the moment they returned to God with their hearts, the heavens would be opened, and the rain would pour down immediately. In a sense, God said, "Let Me watch for a while to see if your repentance is real." God's testing of us is not because God does not know our hearts, but because we do not know them. So during those three months, they were under testing.

Things would be simpler if God's blessings and curses should come so clearly and immediately. If the moment you turned away from God, the curse came, and the moment you returned to God, the blessing came, then there would be no testing by faith. But faith without testing is not precious (see I Peter 1:6-7). So God tested His people for those three months.

In testing, there is another thing involved—God wants to see whether they are looking for God's blessing or looking for God. Yes, God promised to bless, but do they return for blessing or return for the One who blesses? That is where faith is.

Brothers and sisters, where is our faith? When we return to God with our hearts, we expect His blessings.

But His blessings seem to be delayed, and we begin to wonder. Is there not a good lesson here for us? Do we come back for blessings? Or do we come back for God?

That is where the faith of Habakkuk really shined. Oh, I love to read the faith of Habakkuk. I will read it to you:

> For though the fig-tree shall not blossom, neither shall fruit be in the vines; the labour of the olive-tree shall fail, and the fields shall yield no food; the flock shall be cut off from the fold, and there shall be no herd in the stalls: yet I will rejoice in Jehovah, I will joy in the God of my salvation. Jehovah, the Lord, is my strength, and he maketh my feet like hinds' feet, and he will make me to walk upon my high places (3:17-19).

Now, that is faith. On the one hand, we should expect God to bless us, yet on the other hand, our faith should go beyond blessings to God himself. "I will rejoice in the Lord. I will joy in the God of my salvation. The Lord my God is my strength."

Oh, God encouraged His people, built up their faith, and said, "Do not lose faith. It is true. You have been under the hand of discipline through these years. Now you have returned to Me with your heart. I am testing your faith, but I promise you from this day onward, I will bless."

Oh, brothers and sisters, the blessing of the Lord will come for those who remain faithful, pressing on in faith! God first builds up one's faith. Through faith and faithfulness, God's blessing comes. Through God's blessing, there will be much fruit. And with that fruit, God's work shall be done.

Unexpected Blessings

And the word of Jehovah came the second time

God spoke a second time on that same day, the twenty-fourth of the ninth month. When God speaks, He does not speak like man—only once. If He spoke as man, then that would have been the end of the book of Haggai. But God was not satisfied yet. We would think after God had spoken the first time, that was enough. We are promised His blessing. Our faithfulness will be richly rewarded. That is what we are looking for, and we have had it. But God said, "No, no. I have something far bigger and better in view."

> Speak to Zerubbabel, governor of Judah, saying, I will shake the heavens and the earth; and I will overthrow the throne of kingdoms, and I will destroy the strength of the kingdoms of the nations; and I will overthrow the chariots, and those that ride therein; and the horses and their riders shall come down, everyone by the sword of his brother. In that day, saith Jehovah of hosts, will I take thee, Zerubbabel son of Shealtiel, my servant, saith Jehovah, and will make thee as a signet; for I have chosen thee, saith Jehovah of hosts (Haggai 2:21-23).

God spoke again, saying, "This current blessing is but a little foretaste of My blessing." What is the real blessing? *The* blessing of the Lord? "I will shake the heavens and the earth. I will destroy all the nations, the chariots, and the horses. I will take you as My signet, for I have chosen you."

I will take you as My signet, for I have chosen you

The signet here is a signet ring. In the old days, the kings, noblemen, and rich people all wore a signet ring. It was their signature. Their name or initials were carved on that ring. In every contract or document, they stamped a seal on it with their signet ring. That is a signet. We should remember two things about the signet ring:

Inseparable

First, in the old days, a person would never be separated from his signet ring. He kept it and guarded it as his own life. He did not want anyone to steal it and use his signature. The signet represents a person. It represents their name, power, authority, possessions, and inheritance. So in the old days, people hid their signet very carefully. They were inseparable from it. And God said, "I make you My signet. There will be an inseparable relationship between you and Me." In the Song of Solomon, the bride cries out to the bridegroom, "Make me as a signet upon your heart and as a signet ring upon your arm" (see 8:6). In other words, "I will never be separated from your affection; I will never be separated from your strength." It is an inseparable union. That is what is meant by the word signet.

Sealed

And second, when you put the signet on anything, you seal it. Your image is stamped or impressed upon the document or letter.

> In that day ... will I take thee, Zerubbabel son of Shealtiel, my servant and will make thee as a signet (Haggai 2:23).

Naturally, Zerubbabel is but a type of Christ. God looks forward to that day when the kingdoms of the earth shall be destroyed, and the kingdom of Christ shall come and be established. Then everything will bear the mark of Christ. He will openly own everything, and everything will reflect His image. Is this not the blessing of the Lord?—that we should be conformed to His image? He is God's signet.

This word encourages us. He said, "You are Mine. You are not only Mine, but you are also conformed to My image." What blessing can be greater than this? This is God's promise. This is the blessing of the Lord.

Oh, thank God! He promised those who are faithful to Him that He will bless. He will not only bless them with all the spiritual blessings in the heavenlies in Christ Jesus, but He will bless with Christ himself.

There shall be a perfect union—no more separation—forever and forever.

How can we not be built up in faith to finish His work? The Lord has encouraged us. How can we sit back and doubt? Let us press on and, by "faith and patience," inherit our inheritance, the kingdom of God. He has built up our faith; may we go on to please Him and see that His work is done.

Lord, how we praise and thank Thee. Thou art such a great God! Thou hast come to bless us with every spiritual blessing in the heavenlies in Christ. And more than that, Thou dost promise that we shall be conformed to the image of Thy Son, that we shall be joined to Him in one Spirit—never to be separated. O Lord, this is what we look for. Thou hast encouraged us. Thou hast built up our faith that we may go on to please Thee, and to glorify Thee, and to see that Thy work is done. We give Thee all the praise and glory forever and ever in Christ Jesus. Amen.

TITLES AVAILABLE
from Christian Fellowship Publishers
By Watchman Nee

Aids to "Revelation"
Amazing Grace
Back to the Cross
A Balanced Christian Life
The Better Covenant
The Body of Christ: A Reality
The Character of God's Workman
Christ the Sum of All Spiritual Things
The Church and the Work – 3 Vols
The Church in the Eternal
Purpose of God
"Come, Lord Jesus"
The Communion of the Holy Spirit
The Finest of the Wheat – Vol. 1
The Finest of the Wheat – Vol. 2
From Faith to Faith
From Glory to Glory
Full of Grace and Truth – Vol. 1
Full of Grace and Truth – Vol. 2
Gleanings in the Fields of Boaz
The Glory of His Life
God's Plan and the Overcomers
God's Work
Gospel Dialogue
Grace Abounding
Grace for Grace
Heart to Heart Talks
Interpreting Matthew
Journeying towards the Spiritual
The King and the Kingdom of Heaven
The Latent Power of the Soul
Let Us Pray
The Life That Wins
The Lord My Portion
The Messenger of the Cross
The Ministry of God's Word
My Spiritual Journey
The Mystery of Creation
Powerful According to God
Practical Issues of This Life
The Prayer Ministry of the Church
The Release of the Spirit
Revive Thy Work
The Salvation of the Soul
The Secret of Christian Living
Serve in Spirit
The Spirit of Judgment
The Spirit of the Gospel
The Spirit of Wisdom and Revelation
Spiritual Authority
Spiritual Discernment
Spiritual Exercise
Spiritual Knowledge
The Spiritual Man
Spiritual Reality or Obsession
Take Heed
The Testimony of God
The Universal Priesthood of Believers
Whom Shall I Send?
The Word of the Cross
Worship God
Ye Search the Scriptures

The Basic Lesson Series
Vol. 1 - A Living Sacrifice
Vol. 2 - The Good Confession
Vol. 3 - Assembling Together
Vol. 4 - Not I, But Christ
Vol. 5 - Do All to the Glory of God
Vol. 6 - Love One Another

ORDER FROM: 11515 Allecingie Parkway Richmond, VA 23235
www.c-f-p.com

TITLES AVAILABLE
from Christian Fellowship Publishers

By Stephen Kaung

Abiding in God
Acts—The Working of the Holy Spirit
"But We See Jesus"—The Life of the Lord Jesus
Discipled to Christ—As Seen in the Life of Simon Peter
Elijah and Elisha—One Prophetic Ministry
God's Purpose for the Family
Government and Ministry in the Local Church
The Gymnasium of Christ
Haggai
In the Footsteps of Christ
I Corinthians—Called into Fellowship
II Corinthians—*A Man in Christ*
Isaiah—The Redemption of the Lord
The Key to "Revelation" – Vol. 1
The Key to "Revelation" – Vol. 2
The Master's Training
Men After God's Own Heart
Ministering the Word of God
Moses, the Servant of God
Nehemiah—Recovering the Testimony of God
New Covenant Living & Ministry
Now We See the Church—the Life of the Church, the Body of Christ
Proverbs—Wisdom Builds God's House
Recovery
Shepherding
Teach Us to Pray
The Songs of Degrees—Meditations on Fifteen Psalms
The Sons of Korah
The Splendor of His Ways—Seeing the Lord's End in Job
Titus
Worship
Zechariah

The "God Has Spoken" Series
Seeing Christ in the Old Testament, Part One
Seeing Christ in the Old Testament, Part Two
Seeing Christ in the New Testament

ORDER FROM: 11515 Allecingie Parkway Richmond, VA 23235
www.c-f-p.com